Exchange O
Fast Start

Smart Brain Training Solutions

Table of Contents

1. Introduction

Microsoft Exchange is available in on-premises, online and hybrid implementations. With an on-premises implementation, you deploy Exchange server hardware on your network and manage all aspects of the implementation. With an online implementation, you manage the service-level settings, organization configuration, and recipient configuration while relying on Microsoft for hardware and other services. Although an online implementation can be your only solution for all your enterprise messaging needs, a hybrid implementation gives you an integrated online and on-premises solution.

Exchange Online is the subject of this book. Exchange Online is available as part of an Office 365 plan and as a standalone service. Microsoft offers a variety of Office 365 plans that include access to Office Web Apps, the full desktop versions of Office, or both as well as access to Exchange Online. You'll likely want to use an Office 365 midsize business or enterprise plan to ensure Active Directory integration is included as you'll need this feature to create a hybrid Exchange organization. If you don't want to use Office 365, Microsoft offers plans specifically for Exchange Online. The basic plans are the cheapest but don't include in-place hold and data loss prevention features that large enterprises may need to meet compliance and regulatory requirements. That said, both basic and advanced plans support Active Directory integration for synchronization with an on-premises Active Directory infrastructure and the creation of hybrid Exchange organizations.

In Exchange Online, email addresses, distribution groups, and other directory resources are stored in the directory database provided by Active Directory for Windows Azure. Windows Azure is Microsoft's cloud-based server operating system. Exchange Online fully supports the Windows security model and by default relies on this security mechanism to control access to directory resources. Because of this, you can control access to mailboxes and membership in distribution groups and perform other security administration tasks through the standard permission set.

Because Exchange Online uses Windows security, you can't create a mailbox without first creating a user account that will use the mailbox. Every Exchange mailbox must be associated with a user account—even those used by Exchange Online for general messaging tasks.

As you get started with Exchange Online, it's important to keep in mind that available features and options can change over time. Why? Microsoft releases cumulative updates for Exchange on a fixed schedule and applies these cumulative updates to their hosted Exchange servers prior to official release of an update for on-premises Exchange servers. Thus, when you see that an update has been released for the current Exchange Server product you know it has been applied to all Exchange Online servers and all of the mailboxes stored in the cloud as well.

2. Getting Started with Exchange Online

With Exchange Online, the tools you'll use most often for administration are Office Admin Center and Exchange Admin Center. Regardless of whether you use Exchange Online with Office 365, you'll use Office Admin Center as it's where you manage service-level settings, including the Office tenant domain, subscriptions, and licenses.

Navigating Exchange Online Services

When you sign up for Exchange Online, you'll be provided an access URL for Office Admin Center, such as https://portal.microsoftonline.com/admin/default.aspx. After you log in by entering your username and password, you'll see the Office Admin Center dashboard, shown in Figure 1.

> *NOTE*   Throughout this guide, we use screenshots and other images. If you are reading this book in electronic format and the images aren't large enough to view clearly, you have several options. You can try turning your reader on its side and reading in landscape mode, which should help to ensure screenshots and other images are optimally sized. As you'll often be performing tasks on a computer, you also can use a computer in tangent with your e-reader device. Use the computer to follow the discussion by opening the tools or accessing the features being discussed. Use the e-reader device to display the text you are reading.

FIGURE 1 Use the Office Admin Center to manage users and accounts.

From the Office Admin Center dashboard, you'll have full access to Office 365 and Exchange Online. Like Office Admin Center, Exchange Admin Center is a web application. You use Exchange Admin Center to manage:

☐ **Organization configuration data.** This type of data is used to manage policies, address lists, and other types of organizational configuration details.

☐ **Recipient configuration data.** This type of data is associated with mailboxes, mail-enabled contacts, and distribution groups.

Exchange Admin Center is designed to be used with many operating systems and browsers. That said, to ensure all features are available you should use Exchange Admin Center only with supported browser and operating system combinations, which include the following:

☐ With Windows and Windows Server operating systems, use a current version of Internet Explorer, Firefox, or Chrome.

☐ With Mac OS X 10.5 or later use current versions of Firefox, Safari, or Chrome.

☐ With Linux use current versions of Firefox or Chrome.

The easiest way to access Exchange Admin Center, shown in Figure 2, is via Office Admin Center. In Office Admin Center, select Admin and then select Exchange. You'll then be able to work with Exchange recipients, permissions and more.

FIGURE 2 Use the Exchange Admin Center to manage recipients, permissions and more.

After you open Exchange Admin Center, you'll see the list view with manageable features listed in the Feature pane as shown in Figure 3. After you select a feature in the Feature pane, you'll see the related topics or "tabs" for that feature. The manageable items for a selected topic or tab are displayed in the main area of the browser window. For example, when you select Organization in the Feature pane, the topics or tabs that you can work with are: Sharing and Apps.

FIGURE 3 In the list view, manageable features are listed on the left.

The navigation bar at the top of the window has several important options. If there are notifications, you'll see a Notification icon that you can select to display the notifications. The User button displays the name of the currently logged on user. Selecting the User button allows you to logout or sign in as another user.

When working with recipients, you can select More to display additional options, including:

☐ Add or remove columns

☐ Export data for the listed recipients to a .csv file

☐ Perform advanced searches

When you add or remove columns, you can customize the view. Although the settings are saved for the computer that you are using to access Exchange Admin Center, it's important to remember the settings are specific to that computer and browser. As the settings are saved as browser cookies, clearing the browser history will remove the custom settings.

When working with recipients, you usually can select multiple items and perform bulk editing. The key to doing this is to select like items, such as mailbox users or mail-enabled contacts, but not both. Select multiple items using the Shift or Ctrl key and then use bulk editing options in the Details pane to bulk edit the selected items.

Understanding Office 365 Licensing

With Exchange Online, you can perform administration using either the graphical tools or Windows PowerShell. Regardless of which approach you use to create new users in Exchange Online, you must license mailbox users in Office 365. You do this by associating a mailbox plan with each mailbox user.

Using the graphical tools, you can associate mailbox plans when you are creating mailbox users or afterward by editing the account properties. In a remote session with Exchange Online, you can use the –MailboxPlan parameter with the New-Mailbox cmdlet to do the same.

When you assign mailbox plans, you need to ensure you have enough licenses. You purchase and assign licenses using Office 365 Admin Center. Select Licensing in the Feature pane to see the subscription and licensing options. On the Subscriptions tab, select a subscription link to purchase additional licenses for that plan. On the Licenses tab, as shown in Figure 4, you see a summary of the number of valid, expired, and assigned licenses for each plan being used.

FIGURE 4 Use the Licensing node to work with subscriptions and licensing.

Although Office 365 will allow you to assign more mailbox plans than you have licenses for, you shouldn't do this. After the initial grace period, problems will occur. For example, mail data for unlicensed mailboxes may become unavailable. Remember, the number of valid licenses shouldn't exceed the number of assigned licenses.

You activate and license synced users in Office 365 as well. Under Users And Groups > Active Users, select the check boxes for the users you want to activate and license and then select Activate Synced Users. Next, specify the work location for the users, such as United States. Under Assign Licenses, select the mailbox plan to assign. Finally, select Activate.

3. Using Windows PowerShell with Exchange Online

Although Office Admin Center and Exchange Admin Center provide everything you need to work with Exchange Online, there may be times when you want to work from the command line, especially if you want to automate tasks with scripts. Enter Windows PowerShell.

Getting Started with Windows PowerShell

Windows PowerShell is built into Windows and Windows Server. Windows PowerShell supports cmdlets, functions and aliases. Cmdlets are built-in commands. Functions provide basic functionality. Aliases are abbreviations for cmdlet names. As cmdlet, function and alias names are not case sensitive, you can use a combination of both uppercase and lowercase characters to specify cmdlet, function and alias names.

You can work with cmdlets, functions and aliases in several ways. To run a cmdlet, function or alias, you can enter its name at the PowerShell prompt. You also can run cmdlets and functions from scripts and by calling them from C# or other .NET Framework languages.

You use parameters to control the way cmdlets work. All cmdlet parameters are designated with an initial dash (–). As some parameters are position-sensitive, you sometimes can pass parameters in a specific order without having to specify the parameter name. For example, with Get-Service, you don't have to specify the –Name parameter and can simply type:

```
get-service ServiceName
```

where ServiceName is the name of the service you want to examine, such as:

```
get-service MSExchangeIS
```

Here, the command returns the status of the Microsoft Exchange Information Store service. Because you can use wildcards, such as *, with name values, you can also type get-service mse* to return the status of all Microsoft Exchange–related services.

When you work with cmdlets, you'll encounter two standard types of errors: terminating errors and nonterminating errors. While terminating errors halt execution, nonterminating errors cause error output to be returned but do not halt execution. With either type or error, you'll typically see error text that can help you resolve the problem that caused it. For example, an expected file might be missing or you might not have sufficient permissions to perform a specified task.

Although Windows PowerShell has a graphical environment called Windows PowerShell ISE (powershell_ise.exe), you'll usually work with the command-line environment. The PowerShell console (powershell.exe) is available as a 32-bit or 64-bit environment for working with PowerShell at the command line. On 32-bit versions of Windows, you'll find the 32-bit executable in the %SystemRoot%\System32\WindowsPowerShell\v1.0 directory.

On 64-bit versions of Windows and Windows Server, a 64-bit and a 32-bit console are available. The default console is the 64-bit console, which is located in the %SystemRoot%\System32\WindowsPowerShell\v1.0 directory. The 32-bit executable in the %SystemRoot%\SysWow64\WindowsPowerShell\v1.0 directory and is labeled as Windows PowerShell (x86).

With Windows 8 or later, you can start the PowerShell console by using the Apps Search box. Type powershell in the Apps Search box, and then press Enter. Or you can select Start and then choose Windows PowerShell. With Windows 7, you can start Windows PowerShell by selecting Start, pointing to All Programs, Accessories, Windows PowerShell and then selecting Windows PowerShell. From Mac OS X or Linux, you can run either Windows 7 or Windows 8 in a virtual environment to work with Windows PowerShell.

In Windows, you also can start Windows PowerShell from a command prompt (cmd.exe) by typing powershell. To exit Windows PowerShell and return to the command prompt, type exit.

When the shell starts, you usually will see a message similar to the following:

```
Windows PowerShell
Copyright (C) 2012 Microsoft Corporation.
All rights reserved.
```

You can disable this message by starting the shell with the – Nologo parameter, such as:

```
powershell -nologo
```

By default, the version of scripting engine that starts depends on the operating system you are using. With Windows 8.1 and Windows Server 2012 R2, the default scripting engine is version 4.0. To confirm the version of Windows PowerShell installed, enter the following command:

```
Get-Host | Format-List Version
```

Because you can abbreviate Format-List as FL, you also could enter:

```
Get-Host | fl Version
```

> *NOTE* Letter case does not matter with Windows PowerShell. Thus, Get-Host, GET-HOST and get-host are all interpreted the same.

Figure 5 shows the PowerShell window. When you start PowerShell, you can set the version of the scripting engine that should be loaded. To do this, use the –Version parameter. In this example, you specify that you want to use PowerShell Version 3.0:

```
powershell -version 3
```

By default, the PowerShell window displays 50 lines of text and is 120 characters wide. When additional text is to be displayed in the window or you enter commands and the PowerShell console's window is full, the current text is displayed in the window and prior text is scrolled up. To temporarily pause the display when a command is writing output, press Ctrl+S. You can then press Ctrl+S to resume or Ctrl+C to terminate execution.

FIGURE 5 Use the PowerShell console to manage Exchange remotely at the prompt.

Understanding the Default Working Environment

When you run Windows PowerShell, a default working environment is loaded automatically. The features for this working environment come primarily from profiles, which are a type of script that run automatically whenever you start PowerShell. The working environment also is determined by imported snap-ins, providers, modules, command paths, file associations, and file extensions.

To start Windows PowerShell without loading profiles, use the – Noprofile parameter, such as:

```
powershell -noprofile
```

Whenever you work with scripts, you need to keep in mind the current execution policy and whether signed scripts are required. Execution policy is a built-in security feature of Windows PowerShell that controls whether and how you can run configuration files and scripts. Although the default configuration depends on which operating system and edition are installed, policy is always set on either a per-user or per-computer basis in the Windows registry.

You can display the execution policy currently being applied, using the Get-ExecutionPolicy cmdlet. The available execution policies, from least secure to most secure, are:

☐ **Bypass.** Bypasses warnings and prompts when scripts run. Use with programs that have their own security model or when a PowerShell script is built into a larger application.

☐ **Unrestricted.** Allows all configuration files and scripts to run whether they are from local or remote sources and regardless of whether they are signed or unsigned. When you run a configuration file or script from a remote resource, you are prompted with a warning that the file comes from a remote resource before the configuration file is loaded or the script runs.

☐ **RemoteSigned.** Requires all configuration files and scripts from remote sources to be signed by a trusted publisher. However, configuration files and scripts on the local computer do not need to be signed. PowerShell does not prompt you with a warning before running scripts from trusted publishers.

☐ **AllSigned.** Requires all configuration files and scripts from all sources—whether local or remote—to be signed by a trusted publisher. Thus, configuration files and scripts on the local computer and remote computers must be signed. PowerShell prompts you with a warning before running scripts from trusted publishers.

☐ **Restricted.** Prevents PowerShell from loading configuration files and scripts. Effects all configuration files and scripts, regardless of whether they are signed or unsigned. Because a profile is a type of script, profiles are not loaded either.

☐ **Undefined.** Removes the execution policy that is set for the current user scope and instead applies the execution policy set in Group Policy or for the LocalMachine scope. If execution policy in all scopes is set to Undefined, the default execution policy, Restricted, is the effective policy.

By default, when you set execution policy, you are using the LocalMachine scope, which is applied to all users of the computer. You also can set the scope to CurrentUser so that the execution policy level is only applied to the currently logged on user.

Using Set-ExecutionPolicy, you can change the preference for the execution policy. Normally, changes to execution policy are written to the registry. However, if the Turn On Script Execution setting in Group Policy is enabled for the computer or user, the user preference is written to the registry, but it is not effective. Windows PowerShell will display a message explaining that there is a conflict. Finally, you cannot use Set-ExecutionPolicy to override a group policy, even if the user preference is more restrictive than the policy setting. For example, you can set the execution policy to run scripts regardless of whether they have a digital signature and work in an unrestricted environment by entering:

```
set-executionpolicy unrestricted
```

When you change execution policy, the change occurs

immediately and is applied to the local console or application session. Because the change is written to the registry, the new execution policy normally will be used whenever you work with PowerShell.

Working with the Command Path

When you are working with Windows PowerShell, the current directory is not part of the environment path in most instances. Because of this, you typically need to use "./" when you run a script in the current directory, such as:

```
./runtasks
```

Windows PowerShell runs within the context of the Windows command prompt. Although this allows you to run all Windows command-line commands, utilities, and graphical applications from within Windows PowerShell, the Windows PowerShell interpreter parses all commands before passing off the command to the command prompt environment. If Windows PowerShell has a like-named command or command alias, this command or alias is executed and not the expected Windows command. Additionally, if a command doesn't reside in a directory that is part of the PATH environment variable, the command will not run.

The PATH variable also determines where the Windows PowerShell looks for programs and scripts. In Windows

PowerShell, you use $env to work with environment variables. Enter $env:path to view the current settings for the PATH environment variable. Use the followin syntax to add a directory to this variable:

```
$env:path += ";PathToAdd"
```

where PathToAdd is the directory path you want to add to the path, such as:

```
$env:path += ";C:\MyScripts"
```

If you want this directory to be added to the path every time you start Windows PowerShell, add the command as an entry in your PowerShell profile. PowerShell profiles store frequently used elements, including aliases and functions and typically are loaded automatically whenever you work with Windows PowerShell. Keep in mind that cmdlets are built-in and are not affected by the PATH environment variable.

Learning About Cmdlets and Functions

When you are working with Windows PowerShell, you can get a complete list of cmdlets and functions available by entering get-command. The output lists cmdlets and functions by name and associated module.

Another way to get information about cmdlets is to use Get-Help. When you enter get-help *-*, you get a list of all cmdlets, including a synopsis that summarizes the purpose of the cmdlet. Rather than listing help information for all commands, you can get help for specific commands by following Get-Help with the name of the cmdlet you want to work with, such as:

```
get-help clear-history
```

Because Windows PowerShell V3 and later use online and updatable help files, you may see only basic syntax for cmdlets and functions when you use Get-Help. To get full help details, you'll have to either use online help or download the help files to your computer. For online help, add the –online parameter to your Get-Help command, such as:

```
get-help get-variable –online
```

You can use the Update-Help cmdlet to download and install the current help files from the Internet. Without parameters, Update-Help updates the help files for all modules installed on the computer. When you are working with Update-Help, keep the following in mind:

☐ Update-Help downloads files only once a day

☐ Update-Help only installs files when they are newer than the ones on the computer

☐ Update-Help limits the total size of uncompressed help files to 1 GB

You can override these restrictions using the –Force parameter.

4. Connecting to Exchange Online Using PowerShell

The way you use Windows PowerShell to manage Exchange Server and Exchange Online are different. With Exchange Server installations, you manage Exchange using Exchange Management Shell, which is a command-line management interface built on Windows PowerShell that you can use to manage any aspect of an Exchange Server configuration that you can manage in the Exchange Admin Center. With Exchange Online installations, you manage Exchange using a remote session and the built-in functions and capabilities of Exchange Management Shell are not available.

Understanding the Exchange Management Shell

The Exchange Management Shell is designed to be run only on domain-joined computers and is available when you are working with Exchange Server 2013 or later and have installed the Exchange management tools on a management computer or server. The way you start Exchange Management Shell depends on the operating system you are using:

☐ With Windows 7 and Windows Server 2008 R2, you can start Exchange Management Shell by clicking Start, pointing to All Programs, clicking Microsoft Exchange Server 2013, and then clicking Exchange Management Shell.

☐ With Windows 8, Windows 8.1, Windows Server 2012 or Windows Server 2012 R2, you can start Exchange Management Shell by using the Apps Search box. Type shell in the Apps Search box, and then select Exchange Management Shell. Or tap or click Start and then choose Exchange Management Shell.

Whether you are logged on locally to an Exchange server or working remotely, starting Exchange Management Shell opens a custom Windows PowerShell console that runs in a remote session with an Exchange 2013 server. A remote session is a runspace that establishes a common working environment for executing commands on remote computers. Before creating the remote session, this custom console connects to the closest Exchange 2013 server using Windows Remote Management (WinRM) 3.0 and then performs authentication checks that validate your access to the Exchange 2013 server and determine the Exchange role groups and roles your account is a member of. You must be a member of at least one management role.

Because the Exchange Management Shell uses your user

credentials, you are able to perform any administrative tasks allowed for your user account and in accordance with the Exchange role groups and management roles you're assigned. You don't need to run the Exchange Management Shell in elevated, administrator mode, but you can by right-clicking Exchange Management Shell, and then selecting Run As Administrator.

By examining the properties of the shortcut that starts the Exchange Management Shell, you can see the actual command that runs when you start the shell is:

```
C:\Windows\System32\WindowsPowerShell\v1.0\powershell
.exe -noexit -command". 'C:\Program
Files\Microsoft\Exchange
Server\V15\bin\RemoteExchange.ps1';
Connect-ExchangeServer -auto -
ClientApplication:ManagementShell "
```

Here, the command starts PowerShell, runs the RemoteExchange.ps1 profile file, and then uses the command Connect-ExchangeServer to establish the remote session. The – Auto parameter tells the cmdlet to automatically discover and try to connect to an appropriate Exchange server. The – ClientApplication parameter specifies that client-side application is the Exchange Management Shell. When you run the shell in this way, Windows Powershell loads a profile script called RemoteExchange.ps1 that sets aliases, initializes Exchange global variables, and loads .NET assemblies for Exchange. The profile script also modifies the standard PowerShell prompt so that it is scoped to the entire Active Directory forest and defines Exchange-specific functions, including:

☐ **Get-Exbanner.** Displays the Exchange Management Shell startup banner.

☐ **Get-Exblog.** Opens Internet Explorer and accesses the Exchange blog.

☐ **Get-Excommand.** Lists all available Exchange commands.

☐ **Get-Pscommand.** Lists all available PowerShell commands.

☐ **Get-Tip.** Displays the tip of the day.

☐ **Quickref.** Opens Internet Explorer and accesses the Exchange Management Shell quick start guide.

All of these processes simplify the task of establishing an interactive remote session with Exchange server. As implemented in the default configuration, you have a one-to-one, interactive approach for remote management, meaning you establish a session with a specific remote server and work with that specific server whenever you execute commands.

Establishing Remote Sessions

When you are working with PowerShell outside of Exchange

Management Shell, you must manually establish a remote session with Exchange. As the RemoteExchange.ps1 profile file and related scripts are not loaded, the related cmdlets and functions are not available. This means you cannot use Get-Exbanner, Get-Exblog, Get-Excommand, Get-PScommand, Get-Tip or Quickref. Further, as you are working with an online installation of Exchange, the cmdlets available are different from when you are working with Exchange Server.

PowerShell provides several cmdlets for establishing remote sessions, including Enter-PSSession and New-PSSession. The difference between the two options is subtle but important.

Using an Interactive Remote Session

You can use the Enter-PSSession cmdlet to start an interactive session with Exchange or any other remote computer. The basic syntax is Enter-PSSession ComputerName, where ComputerName is the name of the remote computer, such as the following:

```
enter-pssession Server58
```

When the session is established, the command prompt changes to show that you are connected to the remote computer, as shown in the following example:

```
[Server58]: PS C:\Users\wrstanek.cpandl\Documents>
```

While working in a remote session, any commands you enter run on the remote computer just as if you had typed them directly on the remote computer. Generally, to perform administration, you need to use an elevated, administrator shell and pass credentials along in the session. Establishing a connection in this way uses the standard PowerShell remoting configuration.

However, you cannot connect to Exchange Online using the standard PowerShell remoting configuration. You must go through a PowerShell application running on ps.outlook.com or another appropriate web server. Typically, when you work with Exchange Online, you use the connection URI https://ps.outlook.com/powershell/ and the actual session is redirected to your specific online server. To ensure redirection doesn't fail, you must add the –AllowRedirection parameter.

As shown in the following example, you use the –ConnectionURI parameter to specify the connection URI, the –ConfigurationName parameter to specify the configuration namespace, and the –Authentication parameter to set the authentication type to use:

```
Enter-PSSession -ConfigurationName Microsoft.Exchange
-ConnectionUri https://ps.outlook.com/powershell/
-Authentication Basic -AllowRedirection
```

Here, you set the configuration namespace as Microsoft.Exchange, establish a connection to the Exchange Online URL provided by Microsoft, and use Basic authentication. As you don't specify credentials, you will be prompted to provide credentials.

You also can pass in credentials as shown in this example:

```
Enter-PSSession -ConfigurationName Microsoft.Exchange
-ConnectionUri https://ps.outlook.com/powershell/
-Authentication Basic -Credential
wrstanek@imaginedlands.onmicrosoft.com
-AllowRedirection
```

Here, you pass in credentials and are prompted for the associated

password.

Alternatively, you can store credentials in a Credential object and

then use Get-Credential to prompt for the required credentials, as

shown here:

```
$Cred = Get-Credential
Enter-PSSession -ConfigurationName Microsoft.Exchange
-ConnectionUri https://ps.outlook.com/powershell/
-Authentication Basic -Credential
$Cred -AllowRedirection
```

When you are finished working with Exchange Online, you can

end the interactive session by using Exit-PSSession or by typing

exit. Although Enter-PSSession provides a quick and easy way to

establish a remote session, the session ends when you use Exit-

PSSession or exit the PowerShell prompt and there is no way to

reestablish the original session. Thus, any commands you are

running and any command context is lost when you exit the

session.

Thus, as discussed in this section, the basic steps for using a standard interactive remote session are:

1. Open an elevated, administrator Windows PowerShell prompt.

2. Use Enter-PSSession to establish a remote session.

3. Work with Exchange Online.

4. Exit the remote session using Exit-PSSession or by exiting the PowerShell window.

Creating and Importing a Remote Session

Instead of using a standard interactive session, you may want to create a session that you disconnect and reconnect. To do this, you establish the session using New-PSSession and then import the session using Import-PSSession. The basic syntax:

```
$Session = New-PSSession –ConfigurationName
Microsoft.Exchange –ConnectionUri
https://ps.outlook.com/powershell/
–Authentication Basic –Credential
wrs@imaginedlands.onmicrosoft.com
–AllowRedirection
```

In this example, you use New-PSSession to create a session and store the related object in a variable called $Session. You create the session by setting the configuration namespace as Microsoft.Exchange, establishing a connection to the Exchange Online URL provided by Microsoft, which typically is https://ps.outlook.com, and using HTTPS with Basic authentication for the session. You also allow redirection. Allowing redirection is important as otherwise the session will fail when the Microsoft web servers redirect the session to the actual location of your Exchange Online installation.

To establish the connection, you must always pass in your Exchange Online user name and password. In the previous example, you specify the user name to use and are prompted for the related password. You also could specify the credentials explicitly, as shown here:

```
$Cred = Get-Credential
$Session = New-PSSession -ConfigurationName
Microsoft.Exchange
-ConnectionUri https://ps.outlook.com/powershell/
-Authentication Basic -Credential $Cred
-AllowRedirection
```

Here, you store credentials in a Credential object and then use Get-Credential to prompt for the required credentials.

After you establish a session with Exchange Online, you must import the server-side PowerShell session into your client-side session. To do this, you enter the following command:

```
Import-PSSession $Session
```

Where $Session is the name of the variable in which the session object is stored. You can then work with the remote server and Exchange Online.

When you are finished working remotely, you should disconnect the remote shell. It's important to note that, beginning with Windows PowerShell 3.0, sessions are persistent by default. When you disconnect from a session, any command or scripts that are running in the session continue running, and you can later reconnect to the session to pick up where you left off. You also can reconnect to a session if you were disconnected unintentionally, such as by a temporary network outage.

Exchange Online allows each administrative account to have up to three simultaneous connections to sever-side sessions. If you close the PowerShell window without disconnecting from the session, the connection remains open for 15 minutes and then disconnects automatically.

To disconnect a session manually without stopping commands or releasing resources, you can use Disconnect-PSSession, as shown in this example:

```
Disconnect-PSSession $Session
```

Here, the $Session object was instantiated when you created the session and you disconnect while the session continues to be active. As long as you don't exit the PowerShell window in which this object was created, you can use this object to reconnect to the session by entering:

```
Connect-PSSession $Session
```

Later, when you are finished working with Exchange Online, you should remove the session. Removing a session stops any commands or scripts that are running, ends the session, and releases the resources the session was using. You can remove a session by running the following command:

```
Remove-PSSession $Session
```

Thus, as discussed in this section, the basic steps for working with an imported session are:

1. Open an elevated, administrator Windows PowerShell prompt.

2. Use New-PSSession to establish the remote session.

3. Import the session using Import-PSSession.

4. Work with Exchange Online. Optionally, disconnect from the session using Disconnect-PSSession and reconnect to the session using Connect-PSSession.

5. Remove the remote session using Remove-PSSession.

5. Connecting to Windows Azure

You can manage the Office 365 service, its settings and accounts using either Office Admin Center and Windows PowerShell. Every account you create in the online environment is in fact created in the online framework within which Office 365 and Exchange Online operate. This framework is called Windows Azure, and like Windows Server, it uses directory services provided by Active Directory.

Before you can manage Office 365, its settings, and accounts from Windows PowerShell, you must install the Windows Azure Active Directory module (which is available at the Microsoft Download Center: http://go.microsoft.com/fwlink/p/?linkid=236297). Any computer capable of running Exchange 2013 or acting as a management computer can run this module. However, there are several prerequisites, including .NET framework 3.51 and the Microsoft Online Services Sign-in Assistant version 7.0 or later. At the time of this writing, the sign-in assistant was available at http://go.microsoft.com/fwlink/?LinkId=286152. Be sure to download and install only the 64-bit versions of the module and the sign-in assistant.

After you download and install the required components, the Windows Azure Active Directory module is available for your use in any PowerShell window. This module also is referred to as the Microsoft Online module. Although Windows PowerShell 3.0 and later implicitly import modules, you must explicitly import this module with PowerShell 2.0. After you import the module, if necessary, you can connect to the Windows Azure and Microsoft Online Services using the Connect-MSOLService cmdlet.

Because you'll typically want to store your credentials in a Credential object rather than be prompted for them, the complete procedure to connect to Microsoft Online Services by using Windows PowerShell 2.0 is:

```
import-module msonline
$cred = get-credential
connect-msolservice -credential:$cred
```

Or, with Windows PowerShell 3.0, use:

```
$cred = get-credential
connect-msolservice -credential:$cred
```

After connecting to the service, you can use cmdlets for Windows Azure Active Directory to manage online settings and objects. For example, if you want to get a list of user accounts that have been created in the online service along with their licensing status, enter get-msoluser. The results will be similar to the following:

UserPrincipalName	DisplayName	isLicensed
-----------------	-----------	----------
wrstanek@imaginedlands.onm...	William Stanek	True
tonyv@imaginedlands.onm...	Tony Vidal	False

Cmdlets for Windows Azure Active Directory

Exchange Online runs on Windows Azure rather than Windows Server. As the two operating environments have different directory services, you must use cmdlets specific to Active Directory for Windows Azure if you want to work with users, groups and related objects.

You'll find complete information about these cmdlets online at http://msdn.microsoft.com/library/azure/jj151815.aspx. The available cmdlets include:

☐ **Cmdlets for managing groups and roles**

Add-MsolGroupMember

Add-MsolRoleMember

Get-MsolGroup

Get-MsolGroupMember

Get-MsolRole

Get-MsolRoleMember

Get-MsolUserRole

New-MsolGroup

Redo-MsolProvisionGroup

Remove-MsolGroup

Remove-MsolGroupMember

Remove-MsolRoleMember

Set-MsolGroup

☐ Cmdlets for managing licenses and subscriptions

Get-MsolAccountSku

Get-MsolSubscription

New-MsolLicenseOptions

Set-MsolUserLicense

☐ Cmdlets for managing service principals

Get-MsolServicePrincipal

Get-MsolServicePrincipalCredential

New-MsolServicePrincipal

New-MsolServicePrincipalAddresses

New-MsolServicePrincipalCredential

Remove-MsolServicePrincipal

Remove-MsolServicePrincipalCredential

Set-MsolServicePrincipal

☐ Cmdlets for managing users

Convert-MsolFederatedUser

Get-MsolUser

New-MsolUser

Redo-MsolProvisionUser

Remove-MsolUser

Restore-MsolUser

Set-MsolUser

Set-MsolUserPassword

Set-MsolUserPrincipalName

☐ Cmdlets for managing the Azure service

Add-MsolForeignGroupToRole

Connect-MsolService

Get-MsolCompanyInformation

Get-MsolContact

Get-MsolPartnerContract

Get-MsolPartnerInformation

Redo-MsolProvisionContact

Remove-MsolContact

Set-MsolCompanyContactInformation

Set-MsolCompanySettings

Set-MsolDirSyncEnabled

Set-MsolPartnerInformation

☐ Cmdlets for managing domains

Confirm-MsolDomain

Get-MsolDomain

Get-MsolDomainVerificationDns

Get-MsolPasswordPolicy

New-MsolDomain

Remove-MsolDomain

Set-MsolDomain

Set-MsolDomainAuthentication

Set-MsolPasswordPolicy

☐ Cmdlets for managing single sign-on

Convert-MsolDomainToFederated

Convert-MsolDomainToStandard

Get-MsolDomainFederationSettings

Get-MsolFederationProperty

New-MsolFederatedDomain

Remove-MsolFederatedDomain

Set-MsolADFSContext

Set-MsolDomainFederationSettings

Update-MsolFederatedDomain

You also can enter **get-help *msol*** to get a list of commands specific to Microsoft Online Services.

6. Working with Exchange Cmdlets

When you work with Exchange Online, the operating environment is different from when you are working with on-premises Exchange Server installations. As a result, different cmdlets and options are available.

Cmdlets Specific to Exchange Online

Because the operating environment for Exchange Online is different from on-premises Exchange, Exchange Online has cmdlets that aren't available when you are working with on-premises Exchange. You'll find complete information about these cmdlets online at http://technet.microsoft.com/en-us/library/jj200780(v=exchg.150).aspx. The additional cmdlets include:

☐ **Cmdlets for working with online recipients**

Add-RecipientPermission

Get-LinkedUser

Get-RecipientPermission

Get-RemovedMailbox

Get-SendAddress

Import-ContactList

Remove-RecipientPermission

Set-LinkedUser

Undo-SoftDeletedMailbox

☐ Cmdlets for working with connected accounts

Get-ConnectSubscription

Get-HotmailSubscription

Get-ImapSubscription

Get-PopSubscription

Get-Subscription

New-ConnectSubscription

New-HotmailSubscription

New-ImapSubscription

New-PopSubscription

New-Subscription

Remove-ConnectSubscription

Remove-Subscription

Set-ConnectSubscription

Set-HotmailSubscription

Set-ImapSubscription

Set-PopSubscription

☐ Cmdlets for working with antispam and anti-malware

Disable-HostedContentFilterRule

Enable-HostedContentFilterRule

Get-HostedConnectionFilterPolicy

Get-HostedContentFilterPolicy

Get-HostedContentFilterRule

Get-HostedOutboundSpamFilterPolicy

Get-QuarantineMessage

New-HostedConnectionFilterPolicy

New-HostedContentFilterPolicy

New-HostedContentFilterRule

Release-QuarantineMessage

Remove-HostedConnectionFilterPolicy

Remove-HostedContentFilterPolicy

Remove-HostedContentFilterRule

Set-HostedConnectionFilterPolicy

Set-HostedContentFilterPolicy

Set-HostedContentFilterRule

Set-HostedOutboundSpamFilterPolicy

□ Cmdlets for working with connectors

Get-InboundConnector

Get-OutboundConnector

New-InboundConnector

New-OutboundConnector

Remove-InboundConnector

Remove-OutboundConnector

Set-InboundConnector

Set-OutboundConnector

☐ Cmdlets for working with messaging policy and compliance

Get-DataClassificationConfig

Get-RMSTrustedPublishingDomain

Import-RMSTrustedPublishingDomain

Remove-RMSTrustedPublishingDomain

Set-RMSTrustedPublishingDomain

☐ Cmdlets for organization and perimeter control

Enable-OrganizationCustomization

Get-PerimeterConfig

Set-PerimeterConfig

☐ Cmdlets for online reporting

Get-ConnectionByClientTypeDetailReport

Get-ConnectionByClientTypeReport

Get-CsActiveUserReport

Get-CsAVConferenceTimeReport

Get-CsConferenceReport

Get-CsP2PAVTimeReport

Get-CsP2PSessionReport

Get-GroupActivityReport

Get-MailboxActivityReport

Get-MailboxUsageDetailReport

Get-MailboxUsageReport

Get-MailDetailDlpPolicyReport

Get-MailDetailMalwareReport

Get-MailDetailSpamReport

Get-MailDetailTransportRuleReport

Get-MailFilterListReport

Get-MailTrafficPolicyReport

Get-MailTrafficReport

Get-MailTrafficSummaryReport

Get-MailTrafficTopReport

Get-MessageTrace

Get-MessageTraceDetail

Get-MxRecordReport

Get-OutboundConnectorReport

Get-RecipientStatisticsReport

Get-ServiceDeliveryReport

Get-StaleMailboxDetailReport

Get-StaleMailboxReport

Although cmdlets specific to Windows Azure Active Directory and Exchange Online itself are available, many of the cmdlets associated with on-premises Exchange continue to be available as well. Primarily, these cmdlets include those that are specific to recipients and mailboxes and do not include those specific to Exchange on-premises configurations or to Exchange server configurations. For example, you can continue to use cmdlets for working with mailboxes, including Disable-Mailbox, Enable-Mailbox, Get-Mailbox, New-Mailbox, Remove-Mailbox, and Set-

Mailbox. However, you cannot use cmdlets for working with mailbox databases. In Exchange Online, mailbox databases are managed automatically as part of the service.

Working with Exchange Cmdlets

When you work with the Exchange Online, you'll often use Get, Set, Enable, Disable, New, and Remove cmdlets. The groups of cmdlets that begin with these verbs all accept the –Identity parameter, which identifies the unique object with which you are working. Generally, these cmdlets have the –Identity parameter as the first parameter, which allows you to specify the identity, with or without the parameter name.

For identities that have names as well as aliases, you can specify either value as the identity. For example, to retrieve the mailbox object for the user William Stanek with the mail alias Williams, you can use any of the following techniques:

```
get-mailbox Williams
get-mailbox -identity williams
get-mailbox "William Stanek"
get-mailbox -identity 'William Stanek'
```

Typicaly, Get cmdlets return an object set containing all related items when you omit the identity. For example, if you enter get-mailbox without specifying an identity, PowerShell displays a list of all mailboxes available (up to the maximum permitted to return in a single object set).

Cmdlets can display output is several different formats. Although all cmdlets return data in table format by default, there are often many more columns of data than fit across the screen. For this reason, you might need to output data in list format.

To output in list format, redirect the output using the pipe symbol (|) to the Format-List cmdlet, as shown in this example:

```
get-mailbox "William Stanek" | format-list
```

Because fl is an alias for Format-List, you also can use fl, as in this example:

```
get-mailbox "William Stanek" | fl
```

With a list format output, you should see much more information about the object or the result set than if you were retrieving table-formatted data.

Note also the pipe symbol (|) used in the examples. When you are working with Windows PowerShell, you'll often need to use the pipe symbol (|) to redirect the output of one cmdlet and pass it as input to another cmdlet. For example, access to remote PowerShell is a privilege for an online user that can be viewed with Get-User and managed with Set-User. To determine whether a particular user has remote shell access, you can enter:

```
Get-User UserID | fl RemotePowerShellEnabled
```

where UserID is the identity of the user to view, such as:

```
Get-User WilliamS | fl RemotePowerShellEnabled
```

If the user should have remote PowerShell access but doesn't currently, you can enable access using the – RemotePowerShellEnabled parameter of Set-User, as shown in this example:

```
Set-User WilliamS -RemotePowerShellEnabled $true
```

If the user has remote PowerShell access but shouldn't, you can disable access byh setting the –RemotePowerShellEnabled to $false, as shown in this example:

```
Set-User TonyG -RemotePowerShellEnabled $false
```

When you work with list- or table-formatted data, you may want to specify the exact data to display. For example, with Get-User, you can display only the user name, display name and remote PowerShell status using:

```
Get-User | Format-Table Name, DisplayName,
RemotePowerShellEnabled
```

If your organization has a lot of users you can prevent the result set from getting truncated by allowing an unlimited result set to be returned, as shown in this example:

```
Get-User -ResultSize Unlimited | Format-Table
Name,DisplayName,RemotePowerShellEnabled
```

With cmdlets that have many properties, you may want to filter the output based on a specific property. For example, to display a list of all users who have remote PowerShell access, you can filter the result set on the RemotePowerShellEnabled property, as shown in the following example:

```
Get-User -ResultSize unlimited -Filter
{RemotePowerShellEnabled -eq $true}
```

Alternatively, you may want to see a list of users who don't have remote PowerShell access. To do this, filter the results by looking for users who have the RemotePowerShellEnabled property set to $False:

```
Get-User -ResultSize unlimited -Filter
{RemotePowerShellEnabled -eq $false}
```

Thank you for purchasing *Exchange Online Fast Start*! We hope you'll look for other *Fast Start* guides from Smart Brain Training Solutions.

Exchange Online

Fast
Start

A Quick Start Guide for Exchange Online,
Office 365 and Windows Azure!

Smart Brain
Training Solutions

XML

Smart Brain
Training Solutions